Begin with a Bee

Liza Ketchum, Jacqueline Briggs Martin, and Phyllis Root

Illustrations by Claudia McGehee

University of Minnesota Press
Minneapolis · London

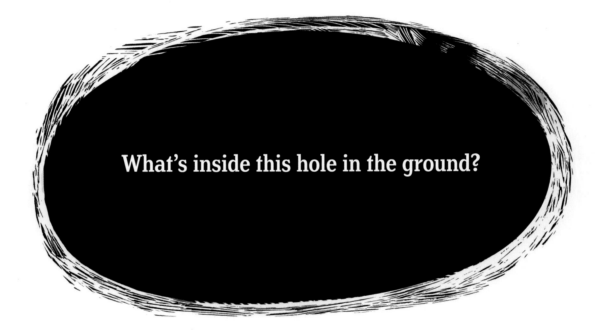

What's inside this hole in the ground?

One bee.

One queen rusty-patched
bumble bee
waiting
all winter long.

And here's the wonder:

her tiny body (not even an inch)
holds everything she needs to create
a whole colony of bees—
this year's bees.

What else waits all winter under the ground?

Seeds and roots
for flowers that bloom early and late,
flowers with nectar and pollen for bees.

Sun shines.
Earth warms.
Seeds and roots
sprout and grow.

Flowers open.

And that one queen rusty-patched bumble bee
crawls from the ground,
flies flower to flower—
maybe plum blossom, wild geranium, shooting star.

What is she searching for?

Nectar and pollen.

She eats, eats, eats,
and eats,
then zigs and zags, flying low.

Where will she nest?

Underground best:
an abandoned mouse burrow, an old mole hole,
or a hollow stump, a fallen tree,
even an empty coat pocket will do.

KEY

QUEEN BUMBLE BEE FLIGHT ---
OVERWINTERING SPOT O
COLONY NESTING SITE X

What will she make when she finds a nest?

All by herself she builds a pot
with wax from her body
and fills it with nectar
for days too cold or rainy to fly
and days when she sits on the eggs she will lay.

All by herself she carries pollen
in the pollen baskets on her back legs.

Once in the nest, she shapes a lumpy pollen ball,
then lays her eggs, seals each egg safe inside.

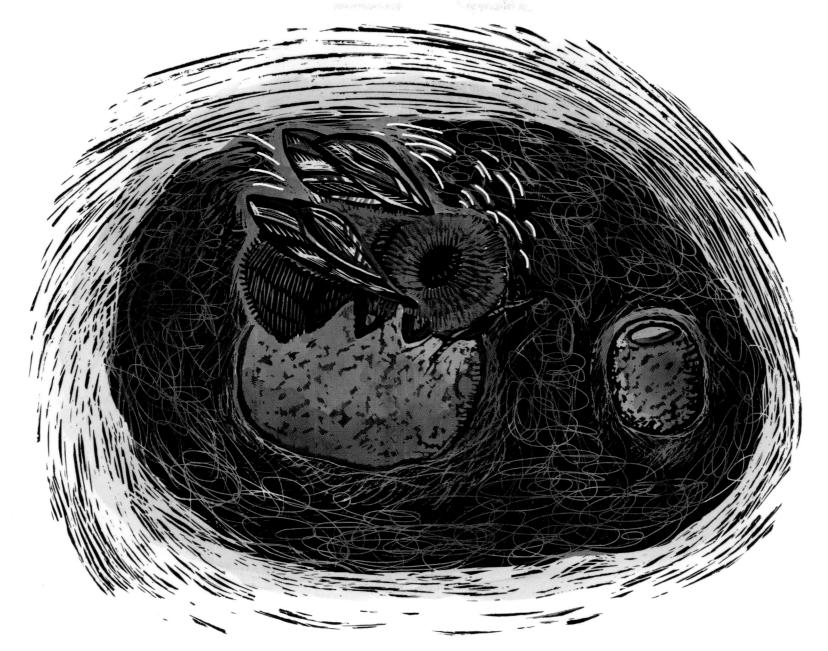

All by herself she sits on the eggs
and shivers to keep them warm.

One day.
Two days.
Three days.
Maybe four days,
maybe five.
Then . . .

Eggs hatch!
Are they bees yet?
No.
Little white grubs,
no eyes, no legs,
eating machines.

All by herself the queen flies,
flower to nest, nest to flower—
wild lupine, wild cherry, serviceberry—
feeding her larvae nectar and pollen.

They grow
and shed their skins
grow and shed
grow and shed
grow until . . .

They poop!
Just once,
then make cocoons with strands of silk
from glands near their mouths.

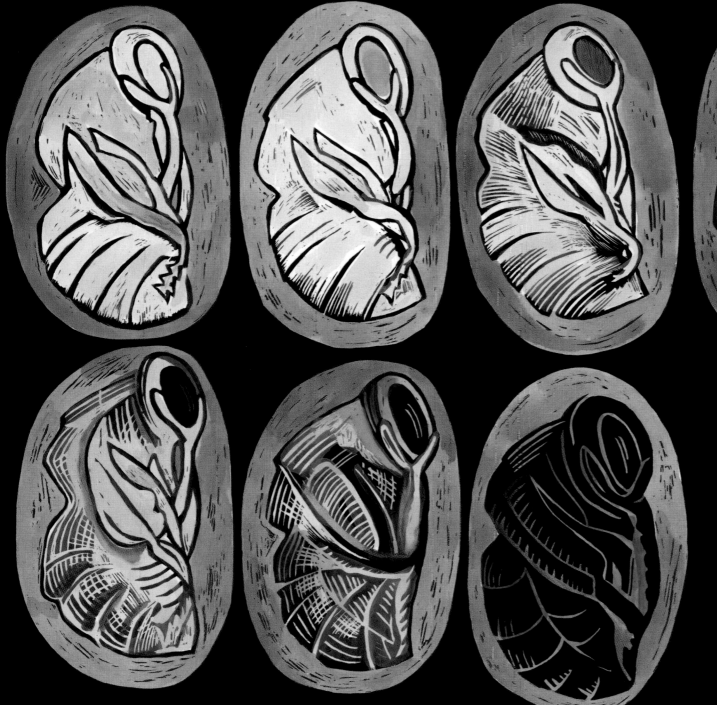

Now are they bees?
Almost.
They're pupae.

One week, two weeks
inside the cocoon,
pupae turning into . . .

finally . . . bees!

Worker bees
(all of them female, none of them queens)
all with a rusty patch on their backs.

Some workers clean the nest.
Some workers fly to find nectar
and pollen to feed the queen.

the QUEEN

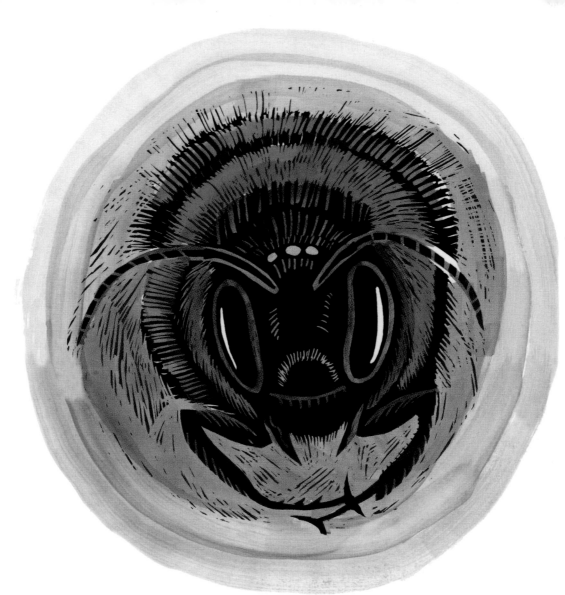

Again and again the queen lays more eggs,
as many as five hundred over the summer.
More eggs, more larvae, more pupae, more worker bees.

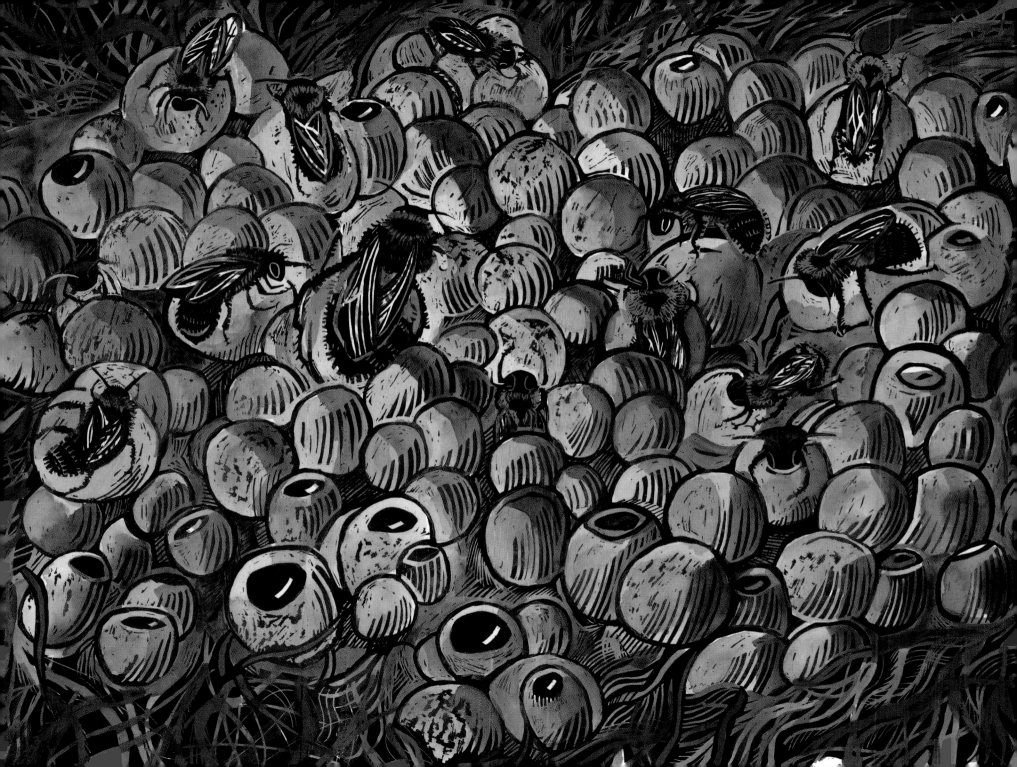

Late in the summer
when goldenrod, gentian,
and aster bloom—

a change.

Now eggs hatch into males
(each with a rusty patch on its back)
and next year's queens.
They fly and mate with bees
from nearby rusty-patched colonies.

Flowers drop seeds,
seeds that started when bumble bees
buzzed the pollen loose from the flowers,
carried it from blossom to blossom—
Joe Pye weed, coneflower, milkweed—

seeds that can sprout
and grow into next year's prairie,
next year's garden.

First frost.
Flowers wither, turn brown,
die back to the ground.
Bee season ends. Bees die, too.

Except . . .

What's inside *this* hole in the ground?

Next year's rusty-patched bumble bee queen.

Seeds drop.
Snow falls.

In the dark hole
all by herself
the new queen hibernates.

She waits for spring,
for the earth to warm.
And here's the wonder:
her tiny body (not even an inch)
holds everything she needs
to create a whole new colony.

Next year's bees

begin with a bee.

The Rusty-Patched Bumble Bee

Furry Bumble Bees

The rusty-patched bumble bee is furry. Its body is covered with short black and yellow hairs.

It is one of about fifty species of bumble bees native to the United States. The native bee families include many other kinds of bees: mason bees, digger bees, sweat bees, carpenter bees. Some bees are as big as your thumb, and other bees are smaller than a grain of rice.

The new rusty-patched queen emerges from her underground nest in early spring. Her colony is one of the last bee colonies to die in autumn. During their lives these bees pollinate thousands of flowers.

What Is Pollination?

Most flowers have petals. At the center of the petals are anthers and stigma. Pollen is on the anthers. If the pollen gets to the stigma, the flower will grow fruit and seeds.

When the bee comes to the flower for nectar and pollen, the bee's movements shake loose some of the pollen on the anthers. That pollen sticks to the bee's furry body. When the bee flies to the next flower, some pollen rubs off on that flower's stigma. Anther to stigma, pollen and bee partner from flower to flower.

Only bumble bees, including the rusty-patched, do buzz pollination: the bees grasp a flower's anthers in their jaws and vibrate their wing muscles to shake loose even more pollen, which causes plants to produce more and bigger fruit. Researchers say that native bees are better pollinators than honeybees, which were imported to this country. Bumble bees pollinate on low-light days, in cool temperatures—even on rainy days, when honeybees might stay in their hives.

Many of the fruits and vegetables we eat depend on bees and other pollinators to reproduce. The next time you eat an apple, a plum, or a tomato sandwich, thank a pollinator, thank a bee.

Will Rusty-Patched Bumble Bees Survive?

Rusty-patched bumble bees are in trouble. For every ten rusty-patched bumble bees that experts found twenty years ago, they now find just one.

Loss of habitat, increased use of pesticides, and climate change have made survival more challenging for rusty-patched bumble bees and other bees.

The wonder of bumble bees—that the queen contains in her body all that is needed to produce a new colony—also threatens their survival. If the one queen dies before establishing a colony, that colony will never exist. There is no spare queen.

In 2017 the rusty-patched bumble bee became the first bee species in the continental United States to be placed on the endangered species list of the U.S. Fish and Wildlife Service. Rusty-patched bumble bees are not the only bees in danger of extinction. Almost 350 bee species vital to pollination are at risk of disappearing.

Ten things we can all do to help:

1. BE a friend to bees no matter where you live. Anyone can BE a gardener! Bees will visit flowers or herbs growing in pots on your city windowsill, fire escape, or balcony.

2. BE a three-season gardener. The rusty-patched bumble bee is a long-season pollinator, so try to have flowers in bloom from early spring through late fall.

3. BE a gardener who plants native plants. Check with gardeners in your area to find out which plants are best for bees where you live. You will attract the "Three Bs": bees, butterflies, and birds.

4. BEware of pesticides and other chemicals that can sicken or kill bees. These chemicals are harmful to humans, too. Your library has good books about how to garden without chemicals.

5. BE messy. Seventy percent of native bees are ground bees, so leave a few spots of tall grass in your yard, as well as a few leaf piles, and maybe a compost heap or areas of undisturbed soil, for spring nests and winter hibernation.

6. BE gentle with bees. Usually bees aren't trying to hurt you, but they may protect their nests.

7. BE loud and tell your friends and neighbors how many plants we depend on that are pollinated by bees: tomatoes, apples, blueberries, almonds, cherries, avocados, cucumbers, onions, grapefruit, oranges, pumpkins, and more!

8. BE a champion of bees. Encourage your city or town to become a Bee City USA. Bee Cities help to create healthy habitats for pollinators. For information, go to www.beecityusa.org.

9. BE an activist. Even if you aren't old enough to vote, you can write a postcard, make a phone call, or email the people who represent you in your local government, in state legislatures, in Congress, and in the White House and tell them to take action to save our native bees and protect our planet. Get your friends to speak out, too.

10. BE a citizen scientist who collects and shares information about the natural world. Keep track in a journal of bees you see or take pictures if you have a camera. When do you see the most bees? Which plants do they like best? Join these groups to learn more and help bees:

• Bumble Bee Watch (www.bumblebeewatch.org) and Bee Spotter (www.beespotter.org) are citizen science databases where you can submit your own bee sightings. Reporting these sightings helps scientists keep track of bee numbers and their range.

• The Great Sunflower Project (www.greatsunflower.org) is a citizen science project that identifies bees when they visit flowers.

• Watch Clay Bolt's wonderful movie about the rusty-patched bumble bee: *A Ghost in the Making: Searching for the Rusty-Patched Bumble Bee* (www.rustypatched.com).

• Join the Xerces Society (www.xerces.org), an organization that protects invertebrates, such as bees, butterflies, and other pollinators. You can download free lists of pollinator plants for your area from this website.

To everyone who loves
native bees.
Love is the first step.
—L.K., J.B.M., P.R.

To Lisa, The B,
and brother Rowan.
—C.M.

The University of Minnesota Press gratefully acknowledges the generous assistance provided for the publication of this book
by the Hamilton P. Traub University Press Fund.

The University of Minnesota Press thanks Oliver, Sebastian, and Augustine Gomez for caring for the bees in their yard and neighborhood.

Published by the University of Minnesota Press
111 Third Avenue South, Suite 290
Minneapolis, MN 55401-2520
http://www.upress.umn.edu

Book design by Brian Donahue / bedesigninc.com

ISBN 978-1-5179-0804-1

Printed in China on acid-free paper

The University of Minnesota is an equal-opportunity educator and employer.

28 27 26 25 24 23 22   10 9 8 7 6 5 4 3 2